ALL ABOARD: THE ULTIMATE GUIDE TO TRAINSPOTTING

From Railway History and Mechanics to
Train Spotters Community and Joy

D.R. T Stephens

S.D.N. Publishing

Copyright © 2023 D.R. T Stephens

All rights reserved

The characters and events portrayed in this book are fictitious. Any similarity to real persons, living or dead, is coincidental and not intended by the author.

No part of this book may be reproduced, or stored in a retrieval system, or transmitted in any form or by any means, electronic, mechanical, photocopying, recording, or otherwise, without express written permission of the publisher.

ISBN: 9798851871320

Cover design by: Art Painter
Library of Congress Control Number: 2018675309
Printed in the United States of America

CONTENTS

Title Page

Copyright

Introduction   1

Chapter 1: The Origins of Trainspotting: The Early Days of Trains, the People Who Loved Them, and th   3

Chapter 2: Anatomy of a Train: Understanding the Different Parts of a Train and How They Work   6

Chapter 3: Train Types and Models: A Closer Look at the Different Types of Trains, Their Unique Char   9

Chapter 4: Famous Train Routes: Delving into the Most Famous Train Routes Around the World, Their Hi   12

Chapter 5: The Trainspotter's Gear: The Basic Equipment Necessary for Trainspotting and How to Use I   15

Chapter 6: Basics of Trainspotting: A Beginner's Guide to Trainspotting, Including Tips and Tricks   18

Chapter 7: Understanding Train Schedules: Learning to Read and Understand Train Schedules, an Essent   21

Chapter 8: Notable Trainspotters: Profiles of Famous Trainspotters and Their Contributions to the Ho   24

Chapter 9: Trainspotting Etiquette: How to Respectfully Engage in Trainspotting   27

Chapter 10: Train Photography: Tips and Techniques for Photographing Trains   30

Chapter 11: Trainspotting and Travel: Combining a Love of Trainspotting with the Desire to Travel — 33

Chapter 12: Trains in Art and Media: Examining the Portrayal of Trains in Film, Literature, and Othe — 36

Chapter 13: Trainspotting in Different Weather Conditions: Challenges and Opportunities for Trainspo — 39

Chapter 14: Trainspotting Challenges: Discussion of Common Challenges Faced by Trainspotters and How — 42

Chapter 15: Safety First: Safety Measures and Precautions to Consider While Trainspotting — 45

Chapter 16: Trainspotting Records: An Exploration of World Records Related to Trains and Trainspotti — 48

Chapter 17: Community and Trainspotting: The Role of Community in Trainspotting, both Locally and Gl — 51

Chapter 18: Trainspotting for Kids: How to Introduce Children to Trainspotting and Make it Fun — 54

Chapter 19: Future of Trains and Trainspotting: Speculations and Facts about the Future of Trains an — 57

Chapter 20: Train Museums and Exhibits: A Tour of Notable Train Museums and Exhibits around the Worl — 60

Chapter 21: Train Simulators and Trainspotting: The Role of Technology and Simulators in the Hobby o — 63

Chapter 22: Career Opportunities in Railways: An Overview of Job Opportunities in the Railway Indust — 66

Chapter 23: Staying Updated: Resources and Methods to Stay Updated on the World of Trains and Trains — 69

Chapter 24: Preserving Train History: The Importance of Train Conservation and Preservation Efforts — 72

Chapter 25: Night Trainspotting: Tips and Techniques for Spotting Trains During the Night — 75

Chapter 26: Collecting Train Memorabilia: Guide to Collecting Train Tickets, Models, and Other Memor — 78

Chapter 27: Online Trainspotting Communities: Introduction to Various Online Platforms and Groups fo   81

Chapter 28: The Role of Trains in History: Exploring How Trains Have Shaped and Changed Societies Th   84

Chapter 29: The Psychological Appeal of Trainspotting: A Deep Dive into Why Trainspotting is a Rewar   87

Chapter 30: The Joy of Trainspotting: A Closing Chapter Celebrating the Simple Joy and Fascination o   90

The End OF the Line!   93

INTRODUCTION

Welcome to the world of trainspotting - a hobby that stretches back to the very advent of railroads, bringing together enthusiasts who find joy, fascination, and a deep sense of satisfaction in observing and studying trains. It's an avocation that resonates with a variety of people, from those intrigued by the romance and history of railways to those who find solace in the methodical and meticulous aspects of identifying and documenting different train models and types.

This book is intended to serve as a comprehensive guide to trainspotting, providing a detailed look into its various facets. It is designed to cater to both the novice, eager to understand the basics of this pastime, as well as the seasoned trainspotter, who may discover new insights and perspectives. We aim to encapsulate the broad spectrum of trainspotting, delving into its historical context, the nitty-gritty of the anatomy of trains, various train types, and their models, as well as an overview of famous train routes globally.

Practical aspects of trainspotting are explored in-depth, including understanding train schedules, employing the right equipment, and the basics of train photography. We also navigate the diverse conditions that trainspotters encounter, from weather challenges to night-time spotting, and discuss the importance of safety.

As you delve deeper, you will be introduced to the remarkable individuals who have made significant contributions to trainspotting and be shown how this hobby fosters a sense of community. In addition, we provide insights into the rich world of train memorabilia, preserving train history, and the role of technology in enhancing the trainspotting experience.

The book further delves into how trainspotting intertwines with other aspects of life, from travel opportunities to potential career paths in the railway industry and even how trains have shaped societies throughout history. We also ponder the future of trains and trainspotting, examining current trends and future predictions.

Towards the end, we strive to shed light on the psychological appeal of trainspotting, exploring why it is such a rewarding hobby for many. Finally, we close with a celebration of the simple joy and fascination of trainspotting – the element that binds all train enthusiasts together.

Whether you are a seasoned trainspotter, a newcomer to the hobby, or simply curious about this unique pastime, this book aims to enlighten, educate, and inspire. So come aboard as we embark on this fascinating journey through the world of trains and those who love to spot them. Here's to the joy of trainspotting!

CHAPTER 1: THE ORIGINS OF TRAINSPOTTING: THE EARLY DAYS OF TRAINS, THE PEOPLE WHO LOVED THEM, AND THE BIRTH OF TRAINSPOTTING AS A HOBBY

The story of trainspotting begins with the story of the train itself, an invention that revolutionized not only transportation but also our relationship with distance, time, and technology. Invented during the early 19th century, the train brought about an age of unprecedented connectivity, making it possible to traverse vast distances in a matter of hours. It reshaped the landscape, not only physically but also culturally and socially.

In the early days, trains were a marvel of modern technology. The steam engine, with its distinctive chugging and whistling, became a symbol of progress, a testament to human ingenuity. Trains held a sense of mystery and adventure; they were a gateway to new places and new experiences. The public was mesmerized, and a deep fascination with trains was ignited. This fascination was the birthplace of trainspotting.

Trainspotting, at its core, is the hobby of observing and documenting trains. It's an interest that can be traced back to the mid-19th century, shortly after the first public railway services started. The first 'trainspotters' were often railway workers who began to notice the distinct characteristics and idiosyncrasies of different locomotives. The variations in design, sound, and speed gave each train its unique personality.

With the spread of railway networks, an increasing number of enthusiasts, who were not necessarily railway workers, began to take an interest in these iron horses. Children and adults alike would stand by railway lines, noting down the numbers and types of passing trains. They would collect and exchange timetables, engine numbers, and other details.

In the U.K., where this hobby first took hold, trainspotters were often seen huddled on platforms, regardless of the weather, jotting down the details of the locomotives. From the thunderous steam engines to the sleek electric trains, every passing carriage held the potential for discovery. The term 'trainspotter' itself didn't come into everyday use until the 1950s, but the activity it describes has a much longer history.

The rise of trainspotting as a recognized hobby was also a product of the industrial era, an era that saw the rise of leisure time. The new working classes, whose hours were not wholly consumed by labor, sought pastimes and hobbies to fill their spare time, and trainspotting emerged as one of these hobbies.

Over the decades, the hobby of trainspotting has evolved, just like the trains themselves. It has weathered the storms of societal change, technological progress, and shifting cultural landscapes. From the steam era to the age of electric and diesel trains, trainspotters have continued their passionate pursuit of knowledge and appreciation of these powerful machines. And while trainspotting may have started in the U.K., it is a hobby that has found followers across the globe, in every country threaded by railway lines.

As we delve deeper into the world of trains and trainspotting in the upcoming chapters, it's essential to remember that this hobby is not just about the trains. It's also about the people who love them, the communities that form around them, and the rich history and culture that they represent. Trainspotting, in essence, is a journey, and as with any journey, it's as much about the journey as it is about the destination.

CHAPTER 2: ANATOMY OF A TRAIN: UNDERSTANDING THE DIFFERENT PARTS OF A TRAIN AND HOW THEY WORK

Before embarking on any pursuit, it is crucial to familiarize oneself with the subject matter at hand. In the context of trainspotting, understanding the anatomy of a train - the various components that come together to create this magnificent mode of transportation - is fundamental.

At the most basic level, a train comprises two primary parts: the locomotive and the carriages or wagons.

The Locomotive

The locomotive, often colloquially referred to as the 'engine,' is the heart of the train. It is responsible for generating the power necessary to move the train. Depending on the era and type of train, this could be a steam engine, a diesel engine, or an electric engine.

A steam locomotive operates on the principle of converting water, heated by burning coal, wood, or oil, into steam. The steam's pressure is then used to drive pistons, which in turn move the wheels.

Diesel locomotives use a diesel engine. The combustion of diesel fuel powers a generator, creating electricity to drive the electric motors that move the wheels.

Electric locomotives are powered by electricity supplied through overhead lines or a third rail. The electricity powers electric motors that drive the wheels.

The Carriages or Wagons

Attached to the locomotive are carriages or wagons. These could serve various purposes: passenger carriages, freight wagons, dining cars, sleeping cars, and more.

Passenger carriages are typically filled with seats and are designed to transport people. They come in different classes, ranging from economy to luxury, each providing a different level of comfort and amenities.

Freight wagons are used for transporting goods. Depending on the type of freight being transported, there are different kinds of wagons, such as open wagons, covered wagons, refrigerator wagons, tank wagons, and flat wagons.

Additional Components

In addition to the locomotive and carriages, there are several other components to a train that trainspotters should be familiar with.

The 'pantograph' is an apparatus mounted on the roof of electric trains to collect power through contact with an overhead line.

The 'coupler' is a mechanism for connecting rolling stock in a train. The design of the coupler is standard over a railway network to ensure compatibility.

The 'bogies' are the framework carrying wheels attached beneath each carriage.

Understanding the anatomy of a train allows trainspotters to appreciate better the technology, design, and sheer engineering prowess that goes into creating these massive vehicles. It provides a foundation upon which they can build their knowledge, identify different types of trains, understand their functions, and appreciate the intricacies of their designs. With this knowledge, a trainspotter can deepen their engagement with their hobby, taking it beyond a mere pastime and transforming it into a profound appreciation for one of humanity's most impactful inventions.

CHAPTER 3: TRAIN TYPES AND MODELS: A CLOSER LOOK AT THE DIFFERENT TYPES OF TRAINS, THEIR UNIQUE CHARACTERISTICS, AND FAMOUS MODELS

Trains come in all shapes and sizes, serving different purposes and operating in various conditions. In this chapter, we'll explore the primary types of trains and some notable models that have marked the history of railways.

Steam Trains

The earliest trains were steam-powered, a technology that revolutionized transportation in the 19th century. These locomotives operate by heating water in a boiler to create steam. The steam pressure then drives the pistons, which, in turn, move the wheels.

Notable model: The 'Flying Scotsman,' a British steam locomotive, has held two world records: one for becoming the first steam locomotive to officially exceed 100 miles per hour and another for the longest non-stop run by a steam locomotive.

Diesel Trains

Diesel locomotives, introduced in the early 20th century, use the combustion of diesel fuel to drive a generator that produces electricity. This electricity then powers motors that turn the wheels. Diesel trains are more efficient and require less maintenance than their steam counterparts.

Notable model: The 'EMD GP7,' a four-axle road switcher diesel-electric locomotive built by General Motors Electro-Motive Division and General Motors Diesel, marked a significant transition in locomotive design.

Electric Trains

Electric trains, powered by electricity supplied through overhead lines or a third rail, are known for their efficiency and environmental friendliness. They are most common in areas with a high volume of train traffic or sensitive ecological conditions.

Notable model: The 'Shinkansen,' or bullet train as it is often described, is a high-speed network of railway lines in Japan. Since its initial launch in 1964, the Shinkansen has transformed rail travel with its impressive speed and safety record.

Freight Trains

Freight trains are designed to transport goods and materials. Depending on the cargo, different types of freight cars may be used, such as boxcars, gondolas, hoppers, tank cars, and flatbeds.

Passenger Trains

Passenger trains transport people between cities, regions, or countries. They range from local commuter trains to long-distance 'Expresses' and luxury trains offering hotel-like amenities.

Notable model: The 'Orient Express,' a long-distance passenger train service created in 1883, was known for its luxurious accommodations and has become synonymous with intrigue and luxury in popular culture.

Light Rail and Trams

Light rail and trams are common in urban areas. These trains are designed for short-distance travel and frequent stops. They often operate both on streets and dedicated tracks.

High-Speed Trains

High-speed trains are passenger trains designed to operate significantly faster than traditional rail traffic. They have an operating speed of over 200 km/h (124 mph).

Notable model: France's 'TGV' (Train à Grande Vitesse) holds the record for the fastest wheeled train, achieving 574.8 km/h (357.2 mph) in 2007.

Recognizing different types of trains and familiar models is a fundamental aspect of trainspotting. Each train has its own unique features, history, and role in the evolution of rail transport. The more you understand these diverse machines, the more enriching your trainspotting experience will be.

CHAPTER 4: FAMOUS TRAIN ROUTES: DELVING INTO THE MOST FAMOUS TRAIN ROUTES AROUND THE WORLD, THEIR HISTORY, AND THEIR SIGNIFICANCE

Throughout history, trains have linked cities, countries, and even continents, providing vital trade connections, accelerating industrialization, and enabling cultural exchange. This chapter will take you on a journey across the globe, exploring some of the most famous train routes, their histories, and why they remain significant today.

Trans-Siberian Railway

Spanning a distance of 9,289 kilometers from Moscow to Vladivostok, the Trans-Siberian Railway is the longest railway line in the world. Opened in phases between 1891 and 1916, this vast route traverses a diverse array of landscapes, from the Ural Mountains to the Siberian steppes and the shores of Lake Baikal, the world's deepest freshwater lake.

Orient Express

Despite its discontinuation as a continuous service, the name Orient Express still echoes luxury and intrigue, largely thanks to its depiction in novels and films. The original route ran from Paris to Istanbul, connecting the west and east. Over the years, the train became synonymous with luxury travel, featuring ornate carriages, gourmet dining, and high-profile passengers.

Indian Pacific, Australia

Australia's Indian Pacific service spans the continent from Perth to Sydney, a journey of over 4,000 kilometers. The train, named for the two oceans it links, offers passengers the opportunity to experience Australia's vast interior landscapes, from the Blue Mountains to the barren Nullarbor Plain.

Rocky Mountaineer, Canada

The Rocky Mountaineer provides one of the most scenic train journeys on earth. It offers several routes through the spectacular Canadian Rockies, with the most popular being the passage from Vancouver to Banff or Jasper. The train travels exclusively in daylight to ensure passengers don't miss any of the breathtaking scenery.

Tokaido Shinkansen, Japan

Japan's Tokaido Shinkansen, often referred to as the bullet train, is a symbol of modernity and efficiency. Operational since 1964, it links Tokyo and Osaka, the country's two most significant metropolitan areas. Apart from its technical prowess, the route offers scenic views of Japan's coastal areas, rural landscapes, and even Mt. Fuji on clear days.

Venice Simplon-Orient-Express, Europe

A modern incarnation of the classic Orient Express, the Venice Simplon-Orient-Express offers a travel experience reminiscent of Europe's golden age of rail travel. The train's route varies but often includes destinations like London, Paris, Venice, and Istanbul. The beautifully restored 1920s carriages, gourmet cuisine, and top-notch service evoke an era of sophisticated luxury.

Rovos Rail's Cape Town to Dar es Salaam, Africa

Rovos Rail, often dubbed 'the Pride of Africa,' offers an epic journey from Cape Town in South Africa to the largest city in Tanzania, Dar es Salaam. This luxurious train navigates diverse landscapes, from the stark beauty of the Namib Desert to the lush greenery of the Zambezi Valley and the dramatic vistas of Victoria Falls.

California Zephyr, USA

Amtrak's California Zephyr links Chicago to San Francisco, taking passengers on a journey through the heartland of America. The route showcases a range of American landscapes, including the Rocky Mountains, the Sierra Nevada, and the expansive plains of Nebraska.

Each of these famous routes tells a story, a journey woven through the fabric of the countries they traverse. Their allure lies in more than just their destinations; it's the journey, the views, the history, and the people that make these routes unforgettable. For the train enthusiast, they represent the very best of what trainspotting can offer.

CHAPTER 5: THE TRAINSPOTTER'S GEAR: THE BASIC EQUIPMENT NECESSARY FOR TRAINSPOTTING AND HOW TO USE IT

Trainspotting, much like any other hobby, requires a specific set of tools to facilitate the best experience possible. In this chapter, we will detail the essential gear needed for trainspotting, provide insights into their importance, and guide you on how to use them effectively.

Notebook and Pen

A notebook is an indispensable tool for trainspotters. It's where you'll jot down observations, note train numbers, times, locations, and other vital details. While a simple pen and paper can suffice, consider investing in a weather-resistant notebook if you plan to spot in all kinds of weather. A pencil can be a practical alternative to a pen, especially in rainy or humid conditions where ink may smudge.

Camera

Capturing a snapshot of a rare locomotive or an iconic train route can be a gratifying part of trainspotting. While a smartphone camera may be enough for casual spotters, a digital camera with a telephoto lens can allow for more professional-looking photos, especially from a distance. Consider a tripod if you're going to capture moving trains to reduce blur.

Binoculars

A quality pair of binoculars can transform your spotting experience, especially when you're positioned far from the tracks. They can help you identify train numbers, models, or any unique characteristics of a train that might be challenging to see with the naked eye.

Portable Chair and Weather Gear

Comfort and preparedness are essential when it comes to trainspotting. A portable, lightweight folding chair can make long spotting sessions much more comfortable. Weather gear like a waterproof jacket, sun hat, or umbrella can keep you prepared for changing weather conditions.

Guidebooks and Timetables

Train guidebooks can provide valuable information, such as the different types of trains, their characteristics, and historical insights. Timetables, on the other hand, can help you plan your spotting sessions to ensure you're at the right place at the right time to spot specific trains.

First Aid Kit

While trainspotting is generally safe, it's always wise to be prepared for minor mishaps. A basic first-aid kit with plasters, antiseptic wipes, and bandages can come in handy. Remember, your safety should always come first.

Food and Water

Train spotting can be a time-consuming hobby, and it's essential to stay hydrated and well-nourished. Carry a reusable water bottle and some snacks to keep your energy levels up.

Smartphone and Apps

In today's digital world, a smartphone can be a valuable tool for trainspotters. There are numerous apps available that provide real-time information about train schedules, types, routes, and even GPS coordinates.

While this list covers the essentials, the gear you decide to bring can be personalized based on your preferences and needs. Remember, the goal is to enhance your trainspotting experience, so choose the tools that will help you enjoy the hobby to its fullest. Happy spotting!

CHAPTER 6: BASICS OF TRAINSPOTTING: A BEGINNER'S GUIDE TO TRAINSPOTTING, INCLUDING TIPS AND TRICKS

Welcome to the world of trainspotting! This chapter will act as a starting point and handbook for those new to the hobby, providing a walkthrough of the basics and sharing helpful tips and tricks to enhance your trainspotting experience.

Understanding Your Interest

First and foremost, it's essential to understand your own interests within trainspotting. Some enthusiasts find joy in photographing trains, while others love the thrill of identifying unique train models. Some may be fascinated by the history of trains, and others might be dedicated to logging as many different train numbers as possible. Your personal interest will guide your trainspotting journey.

Learn About Trains

Armed with a general understanding of what draws you to

trainspotting, it's time to educate yourself about trains. Get familiar with different types of trains, their parts, and their functions. This knowledge will add depth to your hobby and allow you to appreciate the intricacies of trains more fully.

Pick a Spot

Choosing a spot for trainspotting is vital. It can be a local train station, a railway crossing, or a particular part of the train route known for its scenic beauty. Ensure it's a safe, legal, and accessible location where you can watch trains without causing any disturbances.

Train Schedules

Knowing the train schedules for your chosen spot is beneficial. This information will ensure you're there at the right time to spot the trains you're interested in. Many railway companies publish timetables online, making it easy for you to plan your spotting sessions.

Log Your Sightings

Maintain a logbook of your sightings. Note down details such as the train number, model, date and time of spotting, location, and any other interesting observations. This practice not only helps to remember your experiences but also tracks your progress in the hobby.

Join a Community

Connecting with fellow trainspotters can significantly enhance your experience. Join local trainspotting groups or online forums to share experiences, learn from others, and make new friends who share your interest. Remember, trainspotting is not just about the trains; it's also about the community.

Respect the Rules

Safety and respect for rules are paramount in trainspotting.

Always keep a safe distance from tracks, respect private property, and never trespass on railway premises. Respect the privacy of train crew and passengers, and remember, your safety and the safety of others always come first.

Patience and Enjoyment

Trainspotting requires patience, as there can be long waits between sightings. Bring along a book, listen to music, or simply enjoy the peacefulness of your surroundings. The joy in trainspotting often lies in the journey, not just the destination.

Finally, remember that trainspotting is about enjoyment. Whether you're fascinated by the technical aspects of trains, love the history behind them, or simply find watching them pass by soothing, the ultimate goal is to find joy in your hobby. Happy spotting!

CHAPTER 7: UNDERSTANDING TRAIN SCHEDULES: LEARNING TO READ AND UNDERSTAND TRAIN SCHEDULES, AN ESSENTIAL SKILL FOR TRAINSPOTTERS

Having a comprehensive understanding of train schedules is a necessary skill for trainspotters. This knowledge will ensure you make the most out of your trainspotting sessions by helping you be in the right place at the right time. This chapter will guide you on how to read and understand train schedules.

Where to Find Train Schedules

The most obvious place to start looking for train schedules is the website of the relevant railway company. Many railway operators provide detailed timetables for their services online. Additionally, train schedules are usually posted at train stations, in local newspapers, and on dedicated apps for public transportation.

Understanding the Schedule Format

While the specific format may vary by region and railway company, most train schedules typically provide the following key pieces of information:

Train Number or Name: This is usually the unique identifier of the train service.

Departure and Arrival Time: These are the times the train is scheduled to leave the origin station and reach the destination station.

Intermediate Stops: This section lists all the stations the train will stop at between its origin and destination, often with corresponding arrival and departure times.

Days of Operation: This indicates on which days of the week the train runs.

Platform Number: This is the platform at which the train will arrive.

Reading a Train Schedule

Reading a train schedule involves tracing the route of your desired train. First, find the train number or name in the schedule, then follow the corresponding row or column to find out its departure and arrival times, intermediate stops, and days of operation.

Remember that all times are typically presented in a 24-hour format. So, for example, "1500" corresponds to 3 PM. Keep in mind that the schedules usually denote the time when a train is expected to depart from a particular station, except for the final destination, where it's the arrival time.

Punctuality and Delays

Train schedules are designed with a certain amount of slack time to accommodate minor delays, but more significant disruptions may occur due to unexpected incidents. Many railway companies provide real-time updates on their websites or apps about delays, cancellations, or changes to the schedule.

Understanding Train Sequence

In many countries, trains have a specific sequence or order, usually related to the time of the day or the direction of travel. This can help experienced trainspotters predict the arrival of certain types of trains (like freight, express, or local trains) at different times.

By becoming proficient in reading and understanding train schedules, you can plan your trainspotting activities effectively, ensuring you don't miss the trains you're most interested in. Always remember to confirm the schedule closer to your spotting day, as rail services can sometimes change their timetables. Happy spotting!

CHAPTER 8: NOTABLE TRAINSPOTTERS: PROFILES OF FAMOUS TRAINSPOTTERS AND THEIR CONTRIBUTIONS TO THE HOBBY

Trainspotting, as a hobby, has captivated the hearts of many individuals worldwide. It's not only about the appreciation of machinery or the thrill of spotting a rare locomotive; it's also about the community and the stories that come along with it. This chapter will spotlight some notable trainspotters who have elevated the hobby to greater heights through their passion, dedication, and contributions.

1. Pete Waterman:

Pete Waterman, a renowned figure in the British music industry, is an avid trainspotter and railway enthusiast. As one of the U.K.'s most successful music producers, he could often be found indulging in his love for railways during his time off. Waterman also co-founded the London and North Western Railway Heritage, a company devoted to restoring and preserving vintage locomotives, illustrating his commitment to the historical preservation of trains.

2. Michael Portillo:

Former Member of Parliament in the U.K. and television presenter Michael Portillo is another famous face in the trainspotting world. He has presented several railway-themed television series, including "Great British Railway Journeys," "Great Continental Railway Journeys," and "Great American Railroad Journeys." Portillo's work has helped bring trainspotting and the love for railways into the mainstream, bridging the gap between dedicated trainspotters and the general public.

3. Tim Dunn:

Tim Dunn, a railway enthusiast, architectural historian, and presenter, has used his passion to educate others about the wonders of trainspotting. As the host of "The Architecture The Railways Built," Dunn shares his in-depth knowledge of the railway system, helping to keep the interest in trains and trainspotting alive.

4. Ian Marchant:

Ian Marchant, author of the book "Parallel Lines," took his passion for trainspotting to another level. He created a narrative that combined personal memoir with the history and enthusiast culture of trains in the U.K. In doing so, he offered a fascinating look into the world of trainspotting, shedding light on this unique hobby.

These individuals, along with countless other enthusiasts, have showcased that trainspotting isn't just about jotting down numbers in a book. It's about a deep-rooted passion for railways, their history, and their operation. They have also demonstrated that trainspotting can appeal to people from all walks of life, enriching the community with diverse experiences and viewpoints.

Trainspotting is a hobby that has sparked not just interest but also inspiration, as demonstrated by these notable figures. They've used their platforms to share their love for trains, bringing wider attention to the art of trainspotting and showing us that, above all, it is a celebration of passion, curiosity, and lifelong learning.

CHAPTER 9: TRAINSPOTTING ETIQUETTE: HOW TO RESPECTFULLY ENGAGE IN TRAINSPOTTING

Trainspotting, while an exciting hobby, does not exist in a vacuum. It's essential to remember that this activity often takes place in public spaces and around working infrastructure. As such, respecting the rights of others and following safety rules is paramount. This chapter aims to provide you with a set of guidelines for observing the hobby respectfully and responsibly.

1. Respect Railway Property and Boundaries:

Railway infrastructure is not only private property, but it's also a potentially dangerous environment. Trespassing on tracks, sidings, or any other railway property can be illegal and unsafe. Always stay in public areas, respect boundaries, and avoid straying onto railway property.

2. Be Considerate of Others:

Remember, public spaces are shared by everyone, including nontrainspotters. Avoid blocking walkways or views and keep noise to a minimum. If you're in a station, keep in mind that people are often in a hurry, so avoid obstructing their path.

3. Keep a Safe Distance:

Never stand too close to the edge of a platform, and always maintain a safe distance from passing trains. It's not only unsafe but can also be illegal in many areas.

4. Respect Privacy:

When photographing or recording trains, respect the privacy of railway staff and passengers. Do not take close-up photos of individuals without their consent. In some countries, it's illegal to take photos or videos without the subject's consent, even in public places.

5. Leave No Trace:

Whether you're trainspotting in an urban station or a rural spot, ensure you leave the area as you found it. Don't leave litter behind, and if you spot any, consider picking it up. This approach is not just about courtesy; it's about preserving the environment.

6. Follow Local Rules and Regulations:

Different countries and even individual train stations can have their own rules and regulations regarding trainspotting. These can include restrictions on photography, locations where you can stand, and more. Always research local laws and follow them.

7. Be Polite to Railway Staff:

Railway employees are often busy and under pressure. Always be polite and avoid distracting them. If you need help or have questions, wait for an appropriate time and remember to thank them for their time.

Trainspotting is a wonderful hobby that can bring much joy. However, it's crucial to remember that our actions can impact others and the environment. By observing these etiquette guidelines, you'll ensure that you're respecting others, the environment, and the law, ensuring that trainspotting remains a beloved and welcomed activity for everyone.

CHAPTER 10: TRAIN PHOTOGRAPHY: TIPS AND TECHNIQUES FOR PHOTOGRAPHING TRAINS

Train photography is a significant part of the trainspotting hobby for many enthusiasts. A beautifully composed photograph of a locomotive thundering down the tracks can be a joy to behold. It's not just about capturing the image of a train but also about conveying the power, beauty, and elegance of these engineering marvels. This chapter will share some tips and techniques to help you capture stunning train photos.

1. Understanding the Basics of Photography:

To take great train photos, you first need to understand the basics of photography. Familiarize yourself with concepts like shutter speed, aperture, ISO, and composition. Many photography resources can help you learn these basics, and you don't necessarily need an expensive camera to start with. Even modern smartphones can take extraordinary pictures if you know how to use them effectively.

2. Planning Your Shot:

Just like with trainspotting, taking good train photos requires planning. Research the train schedules, find out when the "golden hours" (these are the ones just after sunrise or just before sunset) occur at your chosen spot, consider the background and foreground of your photo, and think about the angle from which you want to capture the train.

3. Safety First:

When choosing your spot, keep safety in mind. Stay off the tracks and ensure you're at a safe distance from the passing train. Do not trespass onto private property, and always be aware of your surroundings.

4. Experiment with Shutter Speed:

One of the critical decisions you'll make when photographing trains is choosing your shutter speed. A faster shutter speed can more effectively freeze the motion of a speeding train, providing a sharp, clear image. On the other hand, a slower shutter speed can blur the train's motion, conveying a sense of speed and power.

5. Play with Perspective:

Try to experiment with various perspectives. Eye-level shots are standard, but low-angle images can make a train seem more imposing. If you can safely and legally do so, higher vantage points can also provide unique views.

6. Include context:

While the train itself is the star of your shot, including the context in your photo can make it more interesting. This could be the station, signals, tracks leading into the distance, or the natural or urban scenery around the train.

7. Be Patient:

Trains operate on schedules, but there can be delays. Plus, you might not nail your shot on the first try. Patience is a virtue in train photography. Be ready to wait for the perfect moment, and be prepared to try again if your initial shots don't turn out as planned.

8. Post-processing:

Finally, learning some basic post-processing techniques can improve your photos significantly. Adjusting exposure, contrast, and saturation, or converting your image to black and white, can add drama and interest to your train photographs.

Remember, the most important thing is to enjoy the process. With time, patience, and practice, you'll develop your own style and technique, capturing stunning images that reflect your passion for trains.

CHAPTER 11: TRAINSPOTTING AND TRAVEL: COMBINING A LOVE OF TRAINSPOTTING WITH THE DESIRE TO TRAVEL

For those who love both trains and travel, the pursuit of trainspotting provides the perfect marriage of these passions. By nature, trains link places and people, often traversing stunning landscapes and connecting dynamic cities. In this chapter, we'll discuss how you can incorporate your love for trainspotting into your travels.

1. Plan Your Destinations Around Train Journeys:

For your next vacation, why not choose a destination famous for its railway heritage or spectacular train journeys? Whether it's the historic steam trains of the U.K., the high-speed bullet trains of Japan, or the scenic Rocky Mountaineer in Canada, there's no shortage of impressive rail experiences around the globe.

2. Explore Train Museums and Exhibits:

Many cities around the world boast museums dedicated to railways and trains. Visiting these can offer you a deep dive into the history and evolution of trains, along with the chance to see rare and famous locomotives. Consider adding destinations like the National Railway Museum in York, UK, or the Railroad Museum of Pennsylvania in the U.S. to your travel itinerary.

3. Join Organized Train Tours:

Several travel companies offer organized tours focused on train travel and trainspotting. These guided tours often provide exclusive access to railways, train yards, and other attractions that might be difficult to arrange on your own.

4. Attend Railfan Events and Festivals:

Throughout the year, various railfan events and festivals take place worldwide. These events often feature historic train rides, model train exhibits, and even photo excursions for train photography. They can also provide an excellent opportunity to congregate with like-minded people who share your passion for trains.

5. Consider the Logistics:

When planning your trainspotting travels, consider practical factors. Pack your gear appropriately - a good pair of binoculars, a camera, a notebook, and suitable clothing for the weather. Don't forget to bring along a railway atlas or guidebook, if available, for your destination.

6. Research Local Trainspotting Etiquette and Regulations:

Rules and norms for trainspotting can vary between countries. In some places, for instance, it might be prohibited to photograph trains or railway infrastructure. Before you go, make sure to research local regulations to avoid any trouble.

7. Embrace the Adventure:

Trainspotting travel isn't just about ticking off locomotives or train routes; it's about embracing the romance and adventure of train travel. Enjoy the landscapes rolling past your window, the rhythm of the wheels on the tracks, and the sheer diversity of people and cultures linked by railway lines.

Trainspotting and travel are a match made in heaven. By planning your trips with an eye for the rails, you can enrich your travel experiences and broaden your trainspotting horizons.

CHAPTER 12: TRAINS IN ART AND MEDIA: EXAMINING THE PORTRAYAL OF TRAINS IN FILM, LITERATURE, AND OTHER MEDIA

The influence of trains extends far beyond transport and industry; they have long been a rich source of great inspiration for artists, writers, and filmmakers. This chapter will delve into the depiction of trains in various forms of media and art, highlighting their symbolism and significance.

1. Trains in Literature:

In literature, trains often serve as powerful metaphors and narrative devices. For instance, they can symbolize change, progress, or transition. From Agatha Christie's classic tale "Murder on the Orient Express," which used the train setting for a thrilling whodunit, to the Hogwarts Express in J.K. Rowling's Harry Potter series, as a bridge between the magical and the mundane, trains hold a significant place in literary landscapes.

2. Trains in Cinema:

The world of cinema, too, has been enthralled by trains. Films like Alfred Hitchcock's "The Lady Vanishes," and "Strangers on a Train," play with suspense and intrigue in a train setting. More recent movies such as "Unstoppable" and "The Polar Express" showcase trains in a thrilling or enchanting light. Whether they're used as action-packed settings, plot devices, or symbols, trains have a unique ability to amplify cinematic narratives.

3. Trains in Painting and Photography:

From the smoky industrial scenes of the 19th-century Realists to the dynamic perspectives of the Futurists, trains have captivated visual artists. They encapsulate movement, power, and human innovation, offering compelling subject matter for artists and photographers. In modern times, train photography has even become a distinct sub-genre of its own, cherished by trainspotters worldwide.

4. Trains in Music:

Trains have also been a popular theme in music, often used to evoke feelings of wanderlust, heartbreak, or freedom. From the American folk tradition with songs like "Midnight Special" or "City of New Orleans," to the rhythm and blues of "Love in Vain" by Robert Johnson, and even in modern pop culture with songs like "Drops of Jupiter" by Train, the evocative power of the train journey resonates across musical genres.

5. Trains in Television and Animation:

Whether it's the quaint charm of Thomas the Tank Engine in children's television or the dystopian train society in "Snowpiercer," trains provide versatile and intriguing contexts in the world of T.V. and animation. They can offer a sense of nostalgia, tension, adventure or even form the backdrop of an entire universe.

The portrayal of trains in art and media often provides a fascinating lens through which we can better understand our relationship with these machines. Beyond their functional role, trains are deeply embedded in our cultural consciousness, representing an array of human experiences and emotions. Their continual appearance across art forms speaks to the enduring fascination we have with these symbols of adventure, progress, and connection.

CHAPTER 13: TRAINSPOTTING IN DIFFERENT WEATHER CONDITIONS: CHALLENGES AND OPPORTUNITIES FOR TRAINSPOTTING IN DIFFERENT CLIMATES AND SEASONS

Engaging in trainspotting under various weather conditions brings about both unique challenges and opportunities. This chapter will explore how different climates and seasons can affect trainspotting and how to adjust your spotting techniques and strategies accordingly.

1. Sunny and Clear Weather:

This is the ideal weather condition for trainspotting. Clear visibility enables you to see far down the tracks and take clear, well-lit photographs. Remember to wear a hat or sunglasses for protection against the sun.

2. Rainy Weather:

Rainy conditions can make trainspotting challenging but also offer unique photo opportunities, such as capturing reflections in puddles or raindrops on train windows. Ensure your equipment is weather-sealed or protected with rain covers. Dress appropriately and consider a sturdy umbrella or waterproof gazebo for long spotting sessions.

3. Snowy Weather:

Trains against a snowy backdrop can be a stunning sight. However, snow can affect train schedules, so it's crucial to stay updated about potential delays or cancellations. Dress warmly, protect your equipment, and carry some warm drinks to keep the cold at bay.

4. Foggy/Misty Conditions:

Foggy conditions can lend a sense of mystery to your train photographs. However, visibility issues may make trains harder to spot and potentially dangerous if you're too close to the tracks. Be cautious and make sure you're always safe.

5. Autumn/Fall Season:

Autumn can provide a beautiful, colorful backdrop for trainspotting. However, falling leaves on the track can sometimes affect train schedules, particularly in areas known for 'leaf fall' delays.

6. Night Time:

While more challenging, night-time trainspotting has its own allure, with lit-up trains contrasting against the dark. Safety is paramount when trainspotting at night; ensure you are visible, stay in well-lit areas, and consider using a tripod for steady low-light photography.

7. Extreme Climates:

For those venturing into more extreme climates, special considerations must be made. In scorching temperatures, ensure you stay hydrated and protected from the sun. In colder climates, frostbite can be a real danger, so warm clothing and heaters are essential.

Regardless of weather conditions, safety should always be your top priority. Be aware of the weather forecast before you head out for trainspotting, and ensure you're prepared with the right gear. Remember, adverse weather can affect train schedules, but it can also offer unique spotting experiences and opportunities for breathtaking photographs.

CHAPTER 14: TRAINSPOTTING CHALLENGES: DISCUSSION OF COMMON CHALLENGES FACED BY TRAINSPOTTERS AND HOW TO OVERCOME THEM

Every hobby comes with its own unique challenges, and trainspotting is no exception. While the pursuit offers numerous rewards and experiences, it is equally important to discuss and address the difficulties trainspotters may encounter. Let's delve into some of these challenges and ways to overcome them.

1. Unpredictable Weather:

As discussed in the previous chapter, weather can significantly impact your trainspotting experience. Sudden rain, snow, or even extreme heat can cut your spotting day short. Always check the forecast before venturing out, pack appropriate gear for the predicted weather, and have a plan B ready.

2. Changing Train Schedules:

Trains may not always adhere strictly to their published schedules due to various reasons like maintenance work, unexpected weather events, or operational issues. Always stay updated with live train schedules from reliable sources, which often have apps or websites for real-time tracking.

3. Limited Visibility:

Trainspotters may struggle with limited visibility due to factors such as fog, darkness, or distant tracks. Proper planning can help to mitigate this - consider the time of day, weather conditions, and bring appropriate equipment like binoculars or a good telephoto lens.

4. Restricted Access:

Trainspotters often grapple with restrictions related to trespassing on railway property. It's crucial to remember that safety and legality are paramount. Always respect boundary signs and do not venture onto active tracks or trespass onto private property.

5. Patience and Time:

Trainspotting requires a significant amount of patience and time, which can be challenging for many. Remember, trainspotting is about enjoying the journey, not just the destination. Bring a book, listen to a podcast, or simply enjoy the surroundings while you wait.

6. Safety Concerns:

As exciting as it may be, trainspotting comes with its own set of safety risks. From staying clear of the tracks to protecting yourself from harsh weather, safety should always be your priority. We'll cover this topic in detail in the next chapter.

7. Negative Stereotypes:

Some people might not understand the appeal of trainspotting and label it as boring or nerdy. Remember, your hobby is for your enjoyment, and you don't need to justify it to others. Join a trainspotting community to connect with like-minded individuals.

8. Cost:

While not the most expensive hobby, trainspotting can still carry costs, such as travel expenses, gear, and potentially accommodation. Budgeting for your hobby and planning in advance can help manage these costs effectively.

Despite these challenges, remember that the joy of trainspotting comes from the love of trains, the thrill of the capture, and the camaraderie between fellow enthusiasts. Every new challenge is another opportunity to learn, grow, and enhance your trainspotting experience.

CHAPTER 15: SAFETY FIRST: SAFETY MEASURES AND PRECAUTIONS TO CONSIDER WHILE TRAINSPOTTING

Ensuring safety while trainspotting is paramount. While the hobby is inherently non-risky when practiced responsibly, certain precautions can never be overemphasized. Here, we discuss essential safety measures that every trainspotter should keep in mind.

1. Respect Railway Boundaries:

This is perhaps the most important safety rule. Never trespass onto railway tracks or other railway property. These areas are meant for authorized personnel only, and trespassing can be extremely dangerous. Remember, a train can come from either direction at any time and is often much quieter and faster than you expect.

2. Stand Back:

Always maintain a safe distance from the tracks. Trains overhang the tracks by at least three feet on either side, and loose straps hanging from rail cars may extend even further. The safe distance provides you with a buffer against any unexpected situations.

3. Be Aware of Your Surroundings:

Keep aware of your surroundings. This means not only watching out for trains but also being mindful of the people around you and any potential hazards in your environment, such as uneven ground, rocks, or other obstacles.

4. Protect Your Hearing:

Trains can be extremely loud, especially if you are standing close by. Consider wearing ear protection if you will be trainspotting for an extended period or if you are sensitive to loud noises.

5. Dress Appropriately:

Wear clothing that is appropriate and suitable for the weather conditions and environment. Dress in layers you can adjust as necessary, and always wear sturdy, comfortable footwear. Bright or reflective clothing can also make you more visible, especially if you are trainspotting in the early morning or late evening.

6. Stay Hydrated and Protected from the Elements:

Bring enough water to stay hydrated, especially during hot weather. Use sunscreen, wear a hat, and take breaks in the shade to protect against sunburn.

7. Carry a First-Aid Kit:

A basic first-aid kit is an essential item for any trainspotter. It should include band-aids, antiseptic wipes, tweezers, and any personal medication you might need.

8. Inform Someone About Your Plans:

Always let someone know where you're going and when you plan to return, especially if you are trainspotting in a remote area. In the event of an emergency, it's vital that someone must know your whereabouts.

9. Use Technology Wisely:

While technology, like smartphones or headphones, can enhance the trainspotting experience, they can also distract. Always ensure that your use of technology doesn't interfere with your awareness of your surroundings.

10. Respect Wildlife:

If you are trainspotting in a rural area, be aware that you are sharing the environment with wildlife. Keep a safe distance, and do not feed or disturb any animals you may encounter.

By adhering to these safety guidelines, trainspotters can ensure their hobby is not only enjoyable but also safe. Always remember, your well-being is paramount, and no photograph or sighting is worth compromising your safety.

CHAPTER 16: TRAINSPOTTING RECORDS: AN EXPLORATION OF WORLD RECORDS RELATED TO TRAINS AND TRAINSPOTTING

In the world of trains and trainspotting, there are countless fascinating records. These records provide a glimpse into the extraordinary and unusual facets of trains and the hobby of trainspotting. In this chapter, we delve into some of the most captivating and intriguing world records related to this field.

1. The Longest Train Ride:

The record for the world's longest direct train ride goes to the "Moscow - Vladivostok" route on the Trans-Siberian Railway. This mammoth journey spans approximately 9,289 kilometers and takes about a week to complete. An adventure of epic proportions, it offers an unparalleled view of Russia's vast and varied landscapes.

2. The Fastest Train:

The title for the world's fastest train is held by the Shanghai Maglev in China. It operates at an impressive top speed of 431 kilometers per hour, which it can achieve due to its magnetic levitation technology that eliminates ground friction.

3. The Heaviest Train:

The record for the heaviest train was set in Australia by BHP, an iron ore company. In June 2001, their train weighed in at a staggering 99,734 tons and was 7.35 kilometers long. The iron ore train consisted of 682 loaded iron ore wagons.

4. The Longest Railway Platform:

The world's longest railway platform can be found in Gorakhpur, India. Measuring 1,366.33 meters long, it holds the Guinness World Record for the longest railway platform, a distinction it has held since October 2013.

5. The Most Trains Spotted in 24 Hours:

The world record for the most trains spotted in a 24-hour period is held by Gary Seymour of the U.K., who spotted an impressive 1,942 trains from the end of platform 1 at Clapham Junction, London, from 19-20 May 1996.

6. Largest Collection of Train Tickets:

The most extensive collection of train tickets is owned by H. Ueda of Japan, who had collected 27,021 different train tickets from around the world as of January 2009.

7. The Oldest Operating Train Station:

The world's oldest continuously operating train station is Broad Green railway station in Liverpool, England. The station was opened in 1830 and has been serving passengers ever since.

8. Largest Model Train Set:

The world record for the largest model train set is held by Miniatur Wunderland in Hamburg, Germany. This incredibly detailed model spans over 15,715 feet of track and includes replicas of various regions around the world.

9. Longest Journey by Train in a Single Country:

The longest journey by train in a single country was achieved by Yijie He (China), who traveled across China for 22,003.98 kilometers (13,670.86 miles) from 31 July to 29 August 2015.

These records not only underscore the vast capabilities of train technology but also the limitless passion and commitment of trainspotters around the globe. Each record represents a unique facet of the incredible world of trains and trainspotting, a world that continues to captivate and fascinate those who delve into its depths.

CHAPTER 17: COMMUNITY AND TRAINSPOTTING: THE ROLE OF COMMUNITY IN TRAINSPOTTING, BOTH LOCALLY AND GLOBALLY

Trainspotting is not just a solitary pursuit. It is a hobby that fosters camaraderie, friendship, and a shared sense of passion and dedication. It is within the community of trainspotters where the magic truly resides, a community that exists both on a local and global scale.

Local Community:

Your local community often plays a crucial role in the realm of trainspotting. Local train clubs and organizations frequently hold meetings, trips, and spotting sessions that bring enthusiasts together. It is within these gatherings that experiences are shared, advice is given, and the joy of trainspotting is celebrated collectively.

Local trainspotters often know the most about their regional train schedules, the best locations for spotting, and the idiosyncrasies of their local railway system. The knowledge shared within these local communities is invaluable, providing a rich source of information for both novice and seasoned spotters alike.

In addition, local train shows and exhibitions are a shared community event that brings enthusiasts together. These events often feature model train displays, historical exhibits, and an array of train-related merchandise that further enhances the trainspotting experience.

Global Community:

The global trainspotting community, thanks to the advent of technology, is a diverse and far-reaching network of individuals united by their shared love for trains. Online forums, social media groups, and trainspotting websites have connected trainspotters from different countries, fostering an international exchange of information and experiences.

The global community enables trainspotters to learn about train systems in different parts of the world, unique train models, and distinct spotting techniques. It provides an opportunity for trainspotters to broaden their knowledge and perspective beyond their local context.

Moreover, the global trainspotting community often organizes international spotting trips and conventions. These events allow trainspotters to meet face-to-face, spot trains in foreign locations, and immerse themselves in the global trainspotting culture.

Importance of Community in Trainspotting:

The sense of community in trainspotting is essential for a number of reasons. Firstly, it creates a support system for trainspotters. When embarking on a new hobby, having a community of like-minded individuals can offer encouragement, guidance, and companionship.

Secondly, the community acts as a repository of shared knowledge and experiences. Within a community, tips are exchanged, insights are provided, and the collective wisdom is enriched.

Thirdly, the community fosters a sense of belonging. It provides a platform where trainspotters can express their enthusiasm, share their successes and challenges, and ultimately connect with others who share the same passion.

In conclusion, whether it's the local club meeting or an international online forum, the role of the community in trainspotting cannot be overstated. It is within these communities that the joy of trainspotting truly comes alive, bridging the gap between individuals and uniting them under the shared banner of a unique and captivating hobby.

CHAPTER 18: TRAINSPOTTING FOR KIDS: HOW TO INTRODUCE CHILDREN TO TRAINSPOTTING AND MAKE IT FUN

Introducing children to trainspotting can be a fun and engaging way to teach them about history, mechanics, and the natural world around them. With the right approach, you can turn a child's curiosity about trains into a life-long passion. Here's how to make trainspotting enjoyable and educational for children:

Start with the Basics:

Children have a natural curiosity, and trains are large, powerful, and exciting, making them naturally attractive to kids. Begin by explaining what trains are, how they work, and what makes them unique. Take them to see trains up close, perhaps at a local train station or a railway museum. The sights, sounds, and movement of trains can be an awe-inspiring experience for a child.

Learn through Play:

Consider getting a model train set for your home. This can help children learn about different types of trains, their components, and the basic concepts of railway infrastructure. Plus, a train set offers hours of imaginative play where kids can build their tracks and scenarios.

Encourage Safe Observation:

Take your child to safe spots where you can observe trains together. Teach them how to notice different types of trains, to listen for their unique sounds, and to spot distinctive features. Always stress the importance of safety around trains, emphasizing that they should never get too close to the tracks.

Make it Interactive:

Create fun activities around trainspotting. This could be sketching or photographing trains, counting the number of carriages on a passing train, or identifying the train type. You could also encourage note-taking of their observations, which helps improve their literacy and analytical skills.

Link it to Travel:

Combine family trips with trainspotting. Traveling by train can be a thrilling experience for children and an excellent opportunity for trainspotting. Whether it's a high-speed intercity train or a quaint countryside railway, each trip presents a chance to learn something new.

Connect with History and Geography:

Trainspotting is an excellent opportunity to teach children about history and geography. Discuss the places trains go, the goods they transport, and how railways have shaped the world. This can make their learning more holistic and interconnected.

Encourage Community Engagement:

If there are local trainspotting groups or events, get your child involved. This can introduce them to a community of like-minded enthusiasts and learn from shared experiences.

Nurture the Passion:

If your child shows continued interest in trainspotting, nurture their passion. Encourage them to read more about trains, watch documentaries, or even play train simulator games. Most importantly, give them the space to explore and enjoy their hobby.

Trainspotting for kids is not just about spotting trains. It's about sparking curiosity, promoting learning, and creating fun family memories. With the right approach, you can make trainspotting a rewarding and enjoyable activity for your child, fostering a hobby they might cherish throughout their lives.

CHAPTER 19: FUTURE OF TRAINS AND TRAINSPOTTING: SPECULATIONS AND FACTS ABOUT THE FUTURE OF TRAINS AND TRAINSPOTTING

The future of trains and trainspotting continues to evolve in exciting ways. The advent of new technology, changing infrastructure, and innovative design all contribute to the dynamic landscape of rail transportation and, by extension, the hobby of trainspotting. This chapter delves into the potential future developments in this fascinating world.

Future of Trains:

High-Speed Rail: High-speed rail systems are set to be the future of intercity travel. Already a common sight in countries like Japan, China, and France, these trains offer fast, efficient, and eco-friendly travel, operating at speeds often exceeding 250 km/h.

Hyperloop: Conceived by Elon Musk, the Hyperloop is a

theoretical transportation system featuring passenger-filled pods traveling through reduced-pressure tubes at high speed. While still in the development phase, the prospect of speeds up to 700 mph is tantalizing and could revolutionize train travel.

Automated Trains: Automation is increasingly prominent in all transport sectors, and trains are no exception. Autonomous trains, guided by GPS and equipped with advanced sensors to detect obstacles, could increase efficiency, safety, and frequency of service.

Green Trains: As the world strives to combat climate change, trains will likely become even greener. Technologies like hydrogen fuel cells or advanced battery systems might replace diesel in locomotives, creating cleaner and more sustainable rail networks.

Future of Trainspotting:

Virtual Trainspotting: With advancements in virtual and augmented reality, virtual trainspotting may become a popular offshoot of the traditional hobby. Enthusiasts could explore trains and rail networks from around the world without leaving their homes.

Drone Trainspotting: Drones offer a new perspective for train photography and videography. As drone technology becomes more accessible, we might see a rise in drone trainspotting, offering a bird's-eye view of the rail action.

Online Communities: The internet already plays a significant role in the trainspotting community, and its influence will only grow. Platforms for sharing photos, knowledge, and experiences will become increasingly sophisticated, connecting trainspotters globally.

Simulator Advancements: Train simulator games are set to become even more realistic, detailed, and immersive, offering enthusiasts new ways to engage with their passion. These advancements may attract a new generation to the hobby.

While speculations about the future of trains and trainspotting are just predictions, they are grounded in current trends and the rapid advancement of technology. The future offers exciting potential for both train technology and the timeless hobby of trainspotting, promising new opportunities for enthusiasts to engage with their passion in novel ways. One thing is certain: trains and trainspotting will continue to adapt and thrive, fueling the fascination of old and new enthusiasts alike.

CHAPTER 20: TRAIN MUSEUMS AND EXHIBITS: A TOUR OF NOTABLE TRAIN MUSEUMS AND EXHIBITS AROUND THE WORLD

For a trainspotter, there's something incredibly magical about wandering through a museum dedicated entirely to trains, marveling at the size, power, and history of these engineering marvels. Train museums and exhibits bring the past to life and give us a glimpse of where the future might take us. In this chapter, we'll embark on a journey through some of the most notable train museums and exhibits across the globe.

1. National Railway Museum, York, United Kingdom:

The National Railway Museum in York is one of the most prominent rail museums globally. It houses over 100 locomotives and almost 200 other items of rolling stock, showcasing several "firsts," including Stephenson's Rocket, the first steam locomotive to run on a public railway, and the futuristic Japanese Shinkansen, also known as the Bullet Train.

2. Smithsonian's National Museum of American History, Washington D.C., USA:

The Smithsonian houses one of the oldest collections, celebrating the rich history of American rail. Among its exhibits, you'll find the John Bull, the oldest operable steam locomotive in the world, and a model of the first American-built steam locomotive, the Tom Thumb.

3. Railway Museum, Saitama, Japan:

This museum chronicles the history of railways in Japan, starting from the steam era to the current Shinkansen (bullet train) era. It's a technologically advanced museum with numerous interactive exhibits, including train simulators and mini train rides for kids.

4. Swiss Museum of Transport, Lucerne, Switzerland:

In addition to aircraft and automobiles, the Swiss Museum of Transport has an impressive collection of railway exhibits. It includes historic Swiss locomotives and a garden railway. It also boasts a fantastic planetarium.

5. Cité du Train, Mulhouse, France:

Europe's largest railway museum, the Cité du Train, offers a fascinating journey through the history of French railways. The museum displays a range of historical French locomotives and rolling stock, including the opulent royal carriages of the 19th century.

6. Rovos Rail, Pretoria, South Africa:

Not just a museum but also an active rail yard, Rovos Rail offers luxury train journeys across Africa and houses an impressive collection of restored carriages and steam engines from the golden age of rail.

7. Museum of the Moscow Railway, Moscow, Russia:

This museum is a window into the history of railways in Russia and the former Soviet Union. Its vast collection includes a replica of Russia's first steam locomotive and a range of royal carriages.

Each of these museums offers unique exhibits, delivering a fascinating blend of history, technology, and culture. They provide an opportunity to step back in time and trace the history of the railways, making them must-visit locations for any trainspotter. A visit to these museums is a celebration of human ingenuity, giving us an appreciation of how far we have come and where we are headed in the world of rail travel.

CHAPTER 21: TRAIN SIMULATORS AND TRAINSPOTTING: THE ROLE OF TECHNOLOGY AND SIMULATORS IN THE HOBBY OF TRAINSPOTTING

Technology has dramatically altered various aspects of our lives, and trainspotting is no exception. One of the most significant advances that have revolutionized this hobby is train simulators. Simulators, for many, are a way to experience the thrill of controlling a train, exploring world-famous rail routes, and deepening their understanding of rail systems without leaving home.

Understanding Train Simulators

Train simulators are software programs designed to recreate the experience of operating a train on a track. They vary in complexity and realism, with some providing a fully immersive, accurateto-life representation of driving a train. The more sophisticated simulators include variables such as weather conditions, signal systems, terrain, and time schedules.

Benefits of Train Simulators for Trainspotters

Train simulators offer a plethora of benefits for trainspotters. They provide a deeper understanding of the operational aspect of trains, which enriches the trainspotting experience. Simulators also allow enthusiasts to explore worldwide rail routes, a treat for those who love combining trainspotting with the desire to travel.

Popular Train Simulators

Train Simulator by Dovetail Games: Known for its realism and extensive range of routes, Dovetail Games' Train Simulator allows players to operate a variety of train types on tracks spanning three continents.

Trainz Simulator by N3V Games: Trainz offers both the experience of operating trains and designing rail systems. The latest versions even support virtual reality for an immersive experience.

Run 8 Train Simulator: Praised for its realistic physics and multiplayer mode, Run 8 offers an authentic train driving experience, including handling freight operations and following signal instructions.

Open Rails: This open-source simulator is compatible with Microsoft's Train Simulator content. Its active development community is continuously working on improvements and updates.

The Future of Train Simulators

The future of train simulators promises even more realistic, immersive experiences. Developments in virtual reality (V.R.) and augmented reality (A.R.) technology are set to enhance train simulators, allowing trainspotters to experience the thrill of driving a train as if they were actually in the cab.

In conclusion, train simulators have transformed trainspotting, adding a new dimension to this fascinating hobby. Whether you are a seasoned trainspotter looking to deepen your understanding of rail operations or a novice looking for an engaging way to start your journey, train simulators offer an accessible, entertaining, and educational experience. They are another testament to the enduring charm of trains and their enduring fascination for millions worldwide.

CHAPTER 22: CAREER OPPORTUNITIES IN RAILWAYS: AN OVERVIEW OF JOB OPPORTUNITIES IN THE RAILWAY INDUSTRY FOR THOSE PASSIONATE ABOUT TRAINS

Trainspotting often begins as a hobby, a passion for the powerful and majestic machines that traverse our world. However, for some, this passion may lead to a career in the railway industry. This chapter aims to outline some of the career opportunities available to those with an enthusiasm for trains.

Engineers and Conductors

The role of a train engineer, also known as a locomotive engineer, is an essential one in the operation of a train. They are responsible for operating the train, following the prescribed routes, schedules, and procedures to ensure the safe and timely transport of passengers or freight.

Conductors, on the other hand, coordinate activities onboard the train. They ensure that passengers have valid tickets, make announcements, and handle any onboard issues that might arise.

Both of these roles typically require specialized training, often provided by the rail company.

Maintenance and Repair

Railway systems require extensive maintenance to ensure their safe operation. This maintenance includes the tracks, the trains themselves, and the various pieces of equipment used in railway operation.

Maintenance roles range from track and signal maintenance to train maintenance and typically involve preventative maintenance and repair work. For those interested in the mechanics and operation of trains, these roles offer an opportunity to work closely with these powerful machines.

Operations and Management

Running a railway involves a vast array of operational and management tasks. These include scheduling, route planning, safety management, and customer service. Operational roles provide an opportunity to ensure the smooth running of the rail system, while management roles involve strategic planning and oversight.

Design and Engineering

For those with an interest in the technical side of railways, careers in design and engineering may be attractive. These roles can involve designing new trains, improving existing designs, developing new railway technologies, or planning and designing new railway routes.

Preservation and Restoration

For those who love the history of railways, roles in preservation and restoration may be appealing. These jobs often involve working with historical railway organizations or museums, preserving old trains and railway equipment, or restoring historical train lines. This work is crucial in preserving the rich history of railways and keeping it alive for future generations.

Tourism and Hospitality

For some, the love of trains intersects with a love of travel or hospitality. Jobs in railway tourism involve running or working on tourist trains, often on historical or scenic railways. These roles can range from being a tour guide to hospitality roles, such as running a dining car.

Conclusion

From hands-on roles to strategic planning, there is enormous potential for a range of career opportunities in the railway industry. If you have a passion for trains, turning this passion into a career can be an incredibly rewarding journey. No matter your skill set or interest, there is likely a role in the railway industry that is a perfect fit for you. It's an opportunity not just to work but to be a part of the world's vibrant and rich railway heritage.

CHAPTER 23: STAYING UPDATED: RESOURCES AND METHODS TO STAY UPDATED ON THE WORLD OF TRAINS AND TRAINSPOTTING

Like any hobby or interest, being informed about the latest developments, news, and resources can significantly enhance your trainspotting experience. This chapter provides a guide to various resources and strategies to stay updated in the world of trains and trainspotting.

Books and Magazines

One of the traditional ways to stay updated on trainspotting is through books and magazines dedicated to the topic. Many publishers release periodicals that discuss the latest news, historical articles, model reviews, and more. These publications often have online counterparts, making them easily accessible to everyone.

Websites and Blogs

Many websites and blogs are dedicated to trains and trainspotting. They can offer a wealth of information, including news articles, photo galleries, forum discussions, and even live railcam feeds. Some blogs are written by experienced trainspotters and can provide valuable insights and advice.

Social Media

Social media apps/platforms such as Twitter, Facebook, Snapchat, TikTok, Instagram, and YouTube have become essential tools for the trainspotting community. They offer opportunities to share experiences, photographs, and videos and to connect with fellow enthusiasts. Many train companies and enthusiast groups have social media profiles where they share updates and news.

Podcasts and Online Videos

Podcasts and online videos offer another avenue to stay updated on trainspotting. There are several podcasts dedicated to trains and railways, where experts discuss various topics, from the history of railroads to the latest technology advancements. YouTube and similar platforms also host many channels dedicated to train content, from trainspotting guides to reviews of model trains.

Train Shows and Events

Train shows, conventions, and events provide an opportunity to meet with fellow enthusiasts, learn about the latest developments, and even buy new equipment or memorabilia. These events are often advertised on social media, in magazines, and on relevant websites.

Mobile Apps

Several mobile apps cater to the trainspotting community. These apps provide real-time train tracking, schedule updates, and even databases of different locomotive models. Some apps cater specifically to trainspotters, featuring logging capabilities, photo sharing, and community forums.

Local Train Clubs and Organizations

Joining a local train club or organization can provide a wealth of information and updates. These groups often hold regular meetings, have newsletters or mailing lists, and offer an excellent opportunity to connect with fellow enthusiasts.

Conclusion

With the advancement of technology, staying updated in the world of trainspotting has become easier than ever. By utilizing a combination of traditional methods like books and magazines, as well as new digital platforms, you can stay informed and connected with the trainspotting community. Remember, the key to a fulfilling trainspotting experience is not just about spotting the most trains but also about continuous learning and sharing your passion with others.

CHAPTER 24: PRESERVING TRAIN HISTORY: THE IMPORTANCE OF TRAIN CONSERVATION AND PRESERVATION EFFORTS

Trainspotting is about more than just the joy of watching and documenting trains. It is a celebration of a rich and intricate history that spans centuries and continents. The preservation of this history is essential not just for future generations of trainspotters but for all those interested in understanding the pivotal role that railways have played in shaping societies. This chapter explores the significance of train conservation and preservation efforts and how these undertakings contribute to the enduring fascination with trains.

The Importance of Preservation

Railways have been a driving force behind industrialization, urbanization, and global connectivity, and trains are tangible relics of this profound history. Preserving these artifacts ensures that we don't lose the physical embodiment of that history. Each train model, railway line, and station has its own story to tell - stories of human ingenuity, perseverance, and the pursuit of progress.

Railway Museums and Historical Societies

Railway museums and historical societies play a crucial role in preserving train history. They acquire, restore, and display vintage locomotives, carriages, and other railway equipment. They also document and curate invaluable historical records, photographs, and memorabilia, providing a glimpse into the railway's rich past.

Restoration Projects

Restoration projects are another critical aspect of train preservation. These projects can range from restoring old railway lines to refurbishing antique train cars. These efforts often involve a blend of dedicated professionals and enthusiastic volunteers who invest time, energy, and resources to bring history back to life.

Educational Initiatives

Preservation isn't just about protecting physical artifacts; it's also about keeping the history and knowledge alive. This is where educational initiatives come in. Schools, museums, and community groups often host workshops, lectures, and field trips focused on railway history, teaching new generations about the significance of trains and railways.

How You Can Contribute

There are many ways you can contribute to preserving train history. Donating to railway museums and historical societies, volunteering in restoration projects, and even simply spreading the word about the importance of preservation are all valuable contributions. As a trainspotter, you can also contribute by documenting and sharing your own observations and experiences.

Conclusion

The preservation of train history isn't just about remembering the past; it's about understanding our present and anticipating our future. The railways have played an integral role in shaping our world, and their impact continues to resonate. By valuing and preserving this history, we ensure that future generations can appreciate the wonder and significance of trains just as we do. Whether you're an avid trainspotter or just someone with an interest in history, remember that every effort to preserve our railway heritage counts.

CHAPTER 25: NIGHT TRAINSPOTTING: TIPS AND TECHNIQUES FOR SPOTTING TRAINS DURING THE NIGHT

As the sun finally sets and darkness envelops the landscape, a different world of trainspotting awakens. Night trainspotting can be a unique and thrilling experience, offering sights and sounds distinct from those of the day. The tracks glisten under the moonlight, the headlamps of the locomotives pierce the night, and the rumbling sounds of the trains seem to carry further in the quiet of the night. This chapter provides an array of tips and techniques to enhance your night trainspotting endeavors.

Understanding the Challenges

The primary challenge of night trainspotting is visibility. Reduced light can make it difficult to spot the trains, let alone identify specific models or capture clear photographs. Additionally, safety can be a concern, particularly in remote or poorly lit locations. Recognizing these challenges is the first step towards overcoming them.

The Right Equipment

Night trainspotting requires some additional gear to that of your daytime hobby. A high-quality flashlight is essential, both for your personal safety and to help identify trains. Consider a headlamp to keep your hands free. For photography, a camera capable of performing well in low-light conditions, coupled with a sturdy tripod, will significantly increase the chances of a clear shot.

Scouting Your Location

Choose your spotting location wisely. You need to be familiar with the area and ensure it is safe to be there at night. Scout during the daylight hours to find a spot that offers a good vantage point and where any potential hazards can be easily identified. Be aware of the train schedule to ensure your night visit will indeed coincide with train movements.

Photographing Trains at Night

Night photography has its own set of rules. Slow shutter speeds can create beautiful light trails, but you will need a tripod to avoid camera shake. Adjust the ISO settings to manage the light sensitivity, but be careful not to set it too high as it can lead to grainy images. Patience and experimentation are key here - night trainspotting photography is an art in itself.

Safety First

Your safety is paramount. Always let someone know where you are going and when you plan to return. Avoid trespassing on the tracks or any restricted areas, even if they offer a perfect view. Wear reflective clothing to be visible to others, and always have a charged mobile phone for emergencies.

Appreciating the Night

Despite its challenges, night trainspotting offers rewards of its own. The quietness of the night amplifies the sounds of approaching trains while the darkness accentuates their lights.

Observing these mighty machines against the backdrop of the night sky brings a sense of wonder, further deepening our appreciation for the world of trains.

Night trainspotting presents its own unique allure. Equipped with knowledge, the right gear, and an appreciation for the beauty of trains under the night sky, you can turn this challenge into a fulfilling experience. As with all aspects of trainspotting, remember to respect the rules, prioritize safety, and treasure the journey of discovery.

CHAPTER 26: COLLECTING TRAIN MEMORABILIA: GUIDE TO COLLECTING TRAIN TICKETS, MODELS, AND OTHER MEMORABILIA

For many enthusiasts, trainspotting extends far beyond the platforms and the thrill of spotting rare locomotives. It extends to collecting train memorabilia, tangible pieces of history that allow them to immerse themselves deeper in their passion. From vintage tickets to intricately detailed models, this chapter serves as a guide to starting and expanding your collection of train memorabilia.

Why Collect Train Memorabilia?

Train memorabilia offer tangible links to history and can bring joy to the collector. Whether it's an antique train lantern, an old railway map, or a model replica of a famous locomotive, each item carries a story that adds depth to the overall trainspotting experience. Furthermore, collecting memorabilia can be a great way to connect with other train enthusiasts and share your passion.

Different Types of Train Memorabilia

Train memorabilia comes in many forms, some of the most common being:

Train Tickets: From vintage paper tickets to modern electronic ones, train tickets can tell a lot about a railway's history, its routes, and its evolution.

Railway Maps and Timetables: These provide insight into the routes, schedules, and the extent of a railway network during different time periods.

Train Models: Miniature replicas of locomotives and carriages are prized for their intricate detailing. These can range from historical steam engines to modern high-speed trains.

Railway Signs and Plates: Vintage signs, station nameplates, and other signage make for distinctive collectibles.

Lanterns and Lamps: Old railway lanterns are popular collectibles, appreciated for their historical significance and industrial aesthetic.

Railway Books and Manuals: From instruction manuals for train operation to books about trains, these provide detailed insights into the world of railways.

Collecting Wisely

As with any form of collecting, there are some guidelines to follow:

Research: Before purchasing an item, research its history, authenticity, and market value. Knowing what you're buying will prevent you from being misled or overpaying.

Condition: The condition of an item significantly influences its value. While some wear and tear can add to an item's charm, severe damage or missing parts can detract from it.

Storage: Proper storage is critical to maintaining the condition and value of your collectibles. Keep them in a safe, dry, and clean environment, away from direct sunlight or extremes of temperature.

Networking: Join trainspotting and memorabilia-collecting communities, both online and offline. These are great places to share your passion, gain knowledge, and find unique pieces for your collection.

Collecting train memorabilia not only enriches your trainspotting experience but also allows you to hold onto pieces of railway history. It's an extension of the love for trains, adding another layer of connection to these marvelous machines and the rich history they represent. Remember, the true joy of collecting lies not in the quantity but in the personal value and satisfaction each piece brings to you.

CHAPTER 27: ONLINE TRAINSPOTTING COMMUNITIES: INTRODUCTION TO VARIOUS ONLINE PLATFORMS AND GROUPS FOR TRAINSPOTTERS

In the digital age, the way hobbies are pursued has evolved. Trainspotting, a traditionally outdoor and solitary pursuit, has also embraced the conveniences of the internet. An online community can provide resources, shared experiences, advice, and a sense of belonging to those who might otherwise pursue their interest in isolation. This chapter introduces various online platforms and groups where trainspotters can connect, learn, and share.

Forums and Discussion Boards

Online forums and discussion boards are a primary source of

interaction and information-sharing for many hobbyists, and trainspotters are no exception. These platforms allow you to ask questions, seek advice, share experiences, and keep abreast of news and updates from the world of railways. Examples include RailUK Forums and TrainNet International.

Social Media Groups

Social media has transformed the way people share their hobbies and passions, and trainspotting is no different. Platforms like Facebook and Instagram are teeming with groups and pages dedicated to trainspotting. Here, members post their spotting experiences, photographs, and videos, making for an engaging and interactive experience. Examples of such communities include 'Trainspotters' on Facebook and the #trainspotting hashtag on Instagram.

Virtual Trainspotting Platforms

Some websites and apps allow trainspotters to log their sightings, helping them keep track of their experiences. Websites like Rail Record and apps like U.K. Train Spotting Log are specifically designed for this purpose, enabling enthusiasts to note down the details of their sightings, such as the locomotive number, location, and date.

Online Simulators and Gaming Communities

For some, trainspotting extends into the virtual world via train simulators. Games like Train Simulator and Trainz offer realistic railway environments where players can operate trains on various routes. These games often have strong online communities where players can exchange tips, share their virtual trainspotting experiences, and even build and share their custom routes and trains.

Webinars and Online Learning Platforms

The internet has become a treasure trove of learning resources, and trainspotting is no exception. Platforms like YouTube host numerous videos that offer insights into different types of trains, railways, and trainspotting techniques. Additionally, webinars and online courses provide structured learning experiences for those wishing to deepen their understanding of trainspotting.

Engaging with online trainspotting communities can be a rewarding experience. These platforms provide the opportunity to learn from others, share your passion, and be part of a community that understands and appreciates your love for trains. Always remember to respect the rules and guidelines of each platform, and be respectful and considerate in your interactions. Happy trainspotting!

CHAPTER 28: THE ROLE OF TRAINS IN HISTORY: EXPLORING HOW TRAINS HAVE SHAPED AND CHANGED SOCIETIES THROUGHOUT HISTORY

Trains have not only played an essential role in the growth of industry and trade but have also left an indelible mark on society's cultural, political, and economic landscape. This chapter explores the transformative role that trains have played throughout history, from promoting the interconnectedness of nations to shaping cities and towns.

Promoting Interconnectedness

Trains played a pivotal role in shrinking distances and promoting a sense of interconnectedness among nations. The transcontinental railroads, for instance, united the East and West coasts of the United States, making cross-country travel possible in a matter of days rather than months. Similarly, the Trans-Siberian Railway connected Moscow to the Far East, facilitating trade and transport across the vast expanses of Russia.

Fueling Industrialization and Economic Growth

Trains were instrumental in fueling the industrial revolution. They provided a fast and reliable means for transporting raw materials to factories and manufactured/finished goods to markets. The expansion of railroads also created jobs, stimulated steel and coal industries, and gave rise to new towns and cities along the routes.

Shaping Cities and Towns

Railroads had a profound impact on urban development. Many cities owe their origins or growth to the railways. Chicago, for instance, grew from a small town to a bustling city primarily due to its role as a major railroad hub. Even today, the influence of railways on urban structure is evident in the central role train stations play in many city centers.

Cultural Influence

Trains have significantly influenced popular culture, including music, literature, and film. From songs like "Folsom Prison Blues" by Johnny Cash to movies like "Murder on the Orient Express," trains have been central themes, reflecting their importance in everyday life. Trains also played a role in the civil rights movement in America, with the 'Freedom Trains' spreading the message of equal rights across the country.

Influencing Timekeeping

An interesting yet often overlooked impact of trains is on timekeeping. Before railways, local times varied from city to city. However, with the introduction of train schedules, a standardized time was needed. This led to the creation of time zones and the concept of 'railway time,' marking a significant shift in how societies managed time.

War and Conflict

Trains played a crucial role in warfare, enabling rapid troop movement and supply of weapons and provisions. The significance of rail transportation was particularly notable in both World Wars, where control over railway networks often determined the outcome of crucial battles.

In conclusion, the influence of trains in history is vast and multifaceted. They have been a driving force of progress, shaping societies in myriad ways. To a trainspotter, understanding this historical impact enriches their appreciation of these magnificent machines and provides a deeper context for their hobby.

CHAPTER 29: THE PSYCHOLOGICAL APPEAL OF TRAINSPOTTING: A DEEP DIVE INTO WHY TRAINSPOTTING IS A REWARDING HOBBY FOR MANY

Trainspotting is more than just a hobby; it is a passion that captivates many across the world. It offers a unique blend of historical interest, technical fascination, and the simple pleasure of observation, all within a community of shared interest. But beyond these reasons, trainspotting has psychological aspects that make it particularly rewarding.

A Pursuit of Knowledge

Trainspotting is a quest for knowledge. Each train model, each railway line has its unique history and technical specifications. The pursuit of this knowledge stimulates intellectual curiosity, providing a continual source of mental engagement that can be deeply satisfying.

Mastery and Achievement

The act of trainspotting involves detailed observation, understanding train schedules, recognizing different train types, and, sometimes, capturing these moments through photography. The sense of mastery that comes with honing these skills over time can contribute to a sense of personal achievement and self-confidence. Not to mention, the thrill of finally spotting a rare train or completing a collection of sightings can be incredibly gratifying.

Mindfulness and Relaxation

Trainspotting requires patience and focus. The act of waiting for trains, observing their details, and immersing oneself in the environment encourages a state of mindfulness. It provides an escape from the regular hustle and bustle, promoting relaxation and reducing stress.

Sense of Community

Being part of a community of trainspotters, whether online or offline, fosters a sense of belonging. Sharing experiences, knowledge, and the common love for trains can create strong social bonds. This connection can bring about feelings of happiness and contentment, enhancing emotional well-being.

Connection to History and Culture

Trains are a vital part of human history and cultural heritage. For many, trainspotting serves as a connection to the past, a link to the great human endeavor of industrialization and progress. This connection can offer a more profound sense of meaning and purpose to the hobby.

The Joy of Collecting

Humans have an innate desire to collect, whether it's stamps, coins, or, in this case, train sightings and memorabilia. The act of collecting provides pleasure, a sense of control, and sometimes, the thrill of the chase. For many trainspotters, building a comprehensive record of train sightings is a profoundly satisfying endeavor.

In conclusion, the appeal of trainspotting extends well beyond a simple interest in trains. It is a multi-faceted hobby that offers intellectual stimulation, emotional satisfaction, a sense of achievement, and much more. These psychological rewards explain why trainspotting continues to captivate people of all ages from all walks of life across the world.

CHAPTER 30: THE JOY OF TRAINSPOTTING: A CLOSING CHAPTER CELEBRATING THE SIMPLE JOY AND FASCINATION OF TRAINSPOTTING

As our journey reaches its terminal station, it's time to reflect on the sheer joy and fascination that trainspotting brings into the lives of its aficionados. Throughout this book, we have journeyed through the captivating world of trains, delving into the historical significance, technical details, and community aspects of this unique hobby. But what ties it all together, and indeed forms the heart of trainspotting, is the profound joy that it brings to those who partake in it.

The Joy of Discovery

The spirit of trainspotting lies in the thrill of discovery. There's the delight that comes from seeing a rare train for the first time or the satisfaction of recognizing a locomotive model based on its unique characteristics. Each day presents a new opportunity for trainspotters to learn, discover, and experience something new and fascinating about the world of trains.

The Pleasure of Observation

Trainspotting isn't just about identifying different trains; it's about the pleasure of observation itself. Watching a train speed down the tracks, hearing the roar of the engines, and witnessing the intricate interplay of machinery in motion is a sensory experience like no other. This simple act of observation can provide a sense of peace, mindfulness, and connection to the larger world.

The Satisfaction of a Passion Pursued

Trainspotting is, at its core, a passion pursued. Like any hobby, it's a commitment of time and energy, but one that brings immense satisfaction. Whether it's staying up late to spot a rare night train, braving harsh weather conditions, or traveling to distant locations to visit train museums and exhibitions, every effort put into this hobby is a testament to a trainspotter's dedication and love for trains.

A Link to the Past and Future

Trains hold a significant place in our collective history, shaping societies, economies, and cultures. Being a trainspotter allows one to feel a deep connection to this rich history, offering a sense of continuity and resonance. Simultaneously, looking toward the future of trains, from high-speed maglev trains to green locomotives, adds an exciting dimension to the hobby.

The Community and Camaraderie

Lastly, the sense of community among trainspotters worldwide is a source of great joy. Sharing sightings, exchanging knowledge, and bonding over a shared interest creates a sense of camaraderie and belonging. It is this collective enthusiasm and friendship that turns a solitary observation into a shared celebration.

In conclusion, the joy of trainspotting comes from the heart. It's in the anticipation of a new sighting, the silence of a quiet platform, the shared stories among fellow enthusiasts, and the continual love for the world of trains. For many, it's more than a hobby—it's a lifelong passion that brings simple, undiluted joy. And it's our hope that through this book, we've managed to share a bit of that joy with you.

As we close this journey, we leave you with a thought: In every passing train, there is a story, a marvel of engineering, a piece of history, and above all, a joy that is waiting to be discovered. Happy trainspotting!

THE END OF THE LINE!